WITHDRAWN

WHAT ARE METAMORPHIC ROCKS?

JUDY MONROE PETERSON

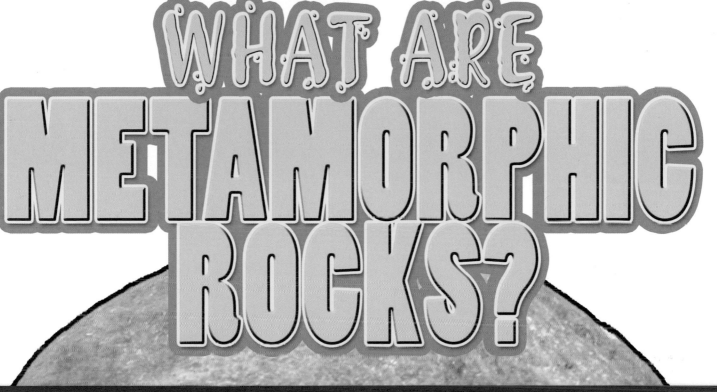

B_____a

Britannica
Educational Publishing

IN ASSOCIATION WITH

ROSEN
EDUCATIONAL SERVICES

Published in 2016 by Britannica Educational Publishing (a trademark of Encyclopædia Britannica, Inc.) in association with The Rosen Publishing Group, Inc.
29 East 21st Street, New York, NY 10010

Distributed exclusively by Rosen Publishing.
To see additional Britannica Educational Publishing titles, go to rosenpublishing.com.

First Edition

Britannica Educational Publishing
J.E. Luebering: Director, Core Reference Group
Mary Rose McCudden: Editor, Britannica Student Encyclopedia

Rosen Publishing
Kathy Kuhtz Campbell: Senior Editor
Nelson Sá: Art Director
Nicole Russo: Designer
Cindy Reiman: Photography Manager
Karen Huang: Photo Researcher

Library of Congress Cataloging-in-Publication Data

Peterson, Judy Monroe, author.
What are metamorphic rocks? / Judy Monroe Peterson. – First edition.
    pages cm. – (Junior geologist: discovering rocks, minerals, and gems)
Audience: Grades 1 to 4.
Includes bibliographical references and index.
ISBN 978-1-68048-243-0 (library bound) — ISBN 978-1-5081-0048-5 (pbk.) — ISBN 978-1-68048-301-7 (6-pack)
1. Metamorphic rocks—Juvenile literature. 2. Geology—Juvenile literature. I. Title.

QE475.P475 2016
552.4—dc23

                                                                                                    2015020775

Manufactured in the United States of America

Photo Credits: Cover, p. 1 © IStockphoto.com/ruksil; cover and interior pages background balounm/Shutterstock.com; p. 4 (left, center) Tyler Boyes/Shutterstock.com; p. 4 (right) elenabum/Shutterstock.com; p. 5 Dchauy/Shutterstock.com; p. 6 DEA/A. Vergani/De Agostini/Getty Images; p. 7 John T Takai/Shutterstock.com; p. 8 LesPalenik/Shutterstock.com; p. 9 De Agostini/Getty Images; p. 10 beboy/Shutterstock.com; p. 11 Spencer Sutton/Science Source/Getty Images; p. 12 Encyclopaedia Britannica, Inc.; p. 13 Doin Oakenhelm/Shutterstock.com; p. 14 Ken M Johns/Science Source/Getty Images; p. 15 Sovfoto/Universal Images Group/Getty Images; p. 16 Dirk Wiersma/Science Source; p. 17 © iStockphoto.com/andyKrakovski; p. 18 Toby Adamson/Axiom Photographic Agency/Getty Images; p. 19 Mint Images/Art Wolfe/Getty Images; p. 20 Joyce Photographics/Science Source/Getty Images; p. 21 Harry Taylor/Dorling Kindersley/Getty Images; p. 22 ultimathule/Shutterstock.com; p. 23 Igor Plotnikov/Shutterstock.com; p. 24 sigur/Shutterstock.com; p. 25 MIXA/Getty Images; p. 26 Universal Images Group/Getty Images; p. 27 Mark Schneider/Visuals Unlimited/Getty Images; p. 28 PHAS/Universal Images Group/Getty Images; p. 29 CreativeNature_nl/iStock/Thinkstock; interior pages (arrow) Mushakesa/Shutterstock.com

CONTENTS

CHANGED ROCK

Rocks are hard materials made up of one or more minerals. Metamorphic rocks are one of the three basic types of rock found on Earth. The other two types are sedimentary and igneous. Metamorphic rock forms from old igneous or sedimentary rock or other metamorphic rock. Very high heat and great pressure

 Rocks make up Earth's land surface. The three main types (from left to right) are igneous, metamorphic, and sedimentary.

inside Earth's crust can change old rock into new metamorphic rocks.

The name "metamorphic" comes from Greek words meaning "change of shape." Most metamorphic rocks form slowly over millions of years. They come in thousands of different shapes, colors, and sizes. Many mountain chains are made of metamorphic rock. People use metamorphic rock, such as gneiss and quartzite, to make building materials. Slate is made into roofing. People make statues and buildings from beautiful marble.

Metamorphic rocks are common in mountain ranges all over the world.

REMAKING ROCKS

Rocks are formed, worn down, and then formed again in a process called the rock cycle. This means rocks can change into other types of rocks. The events of the rock cycle can take place over millions of years.

The process depends on time, temperature, pressure, and changes in conditions under Earth's crust and at its surface.

Vocabulary

The rock cycle is the process by which rocks of one kind change into rocks of another kind. The events of the rock cycle can take place over millions of years. Rocks can follow many paths through the rock cycle.

Mountains may look strong, but they are being worn down into small rocks and sand every day.

The crust is the outer layer of Earth. The lower parts of this layer are solid rock, or bedrock. Broken bits of rock lie on top. The smallest bits of rock make up sand and soil. Underneath Earth's crust is the upper mantle, a thick layer of mostly solid rock. Below that, pools of melted rock, or magma, continuously move inside the lower mantle. Magma is heated from the high temperatures in Earth's core.

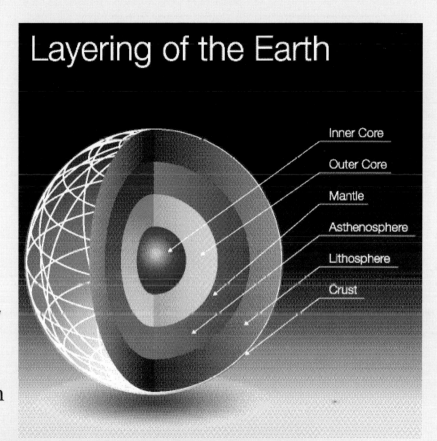

Layering of the Earth

Inner Core

Outer Core

Mantle

Asthenosphere

Lithosphere

Crust

Magma is found in the part of Earth's mantle called the asthenosphere.

UNDER PRESSURE

Metamorphic rocks form when other rocks are affected by temperature and pressure. The outer crust layers are heavy. They put great amounts of pressure on the rocks below. The rocks are pushed down or forced into one another deep in Earth. The rocks are put under so much pressure that their minerals break down. When the minerals mix together again, they form new rock. Pressure increases inside Earth's crust with depth. That is, the rocks that are deepest beneath the surface receive the greatest pressure. The pressure at which metamorphic changes take

Gneiss is one of the most common metamorphic rocks. It has distinct banding caused by great pressure.

Think About It

Why do you think metamorphic rock is usually not formed equally in all directions at any place within Earth's crust?

place is up to thousands of times greater than Earth's atmospheric pressure, or the weight of air in Earth's atmosphere. Eclogitc is a metamorphic rock formed under great pressure.

Eclogite is very tough and strong. It is produced under huge pressure in the mantle.

HIGH HEAT

Metamorphic rocks also form in places where hot, liquid rock called magma flows. Magma is formed

inside Earth and will eventually make its way through the mantle and onto Earth's surface. When magma is forced through the rocks under the surface of Earth, the rocks surrounding the magma become very hot. The increase in temperature causes the rocks to become so hot

When magma reaches Earth's surface, it is called lava. Lava flows out of a volcano.

Compare and Contrast

The rocks closest to magma become very hot and can change into metamorphic rocks. How does this action compare to rocks farther away from magma?

that they change into new and different rocks. This process is called contact metamorphism. Hornfels, a kind of metamorphic rock, is created by contact metamorphism.

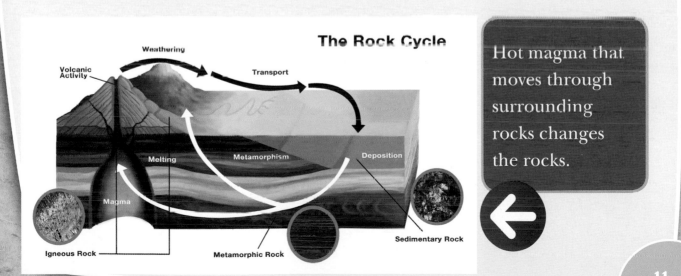

The Rock Cycle

Weathering

Volcanic Activity

Transport

Melting

Metamorphism

Deposition

Magma

Igneous Rock

Metamorphic Rock

Sedimentary Rock

Hot magma that moves through surrounding rocks changes the rocks.

MOVING PLATES

Earth's outer layer is made up of huge pieces of solid rock called plates that are always slowly moving. All of Earth's surface land and water sit on these solid rocks. Under the plates is a layer of mantle that has huge streams of liquid magma buried within it. The plates slide over this mantle layer. Metamorphic rock often forms in places where large sections of plates come together and push against each other creating very high pressure and heat.

Plates travel slowly. Some plates move apart. Other

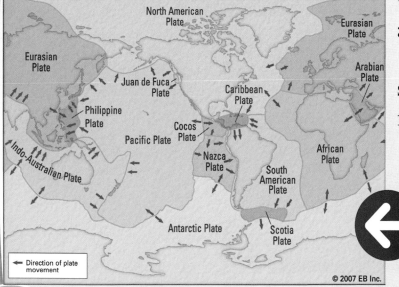

North American Plate

Eurasian Plate

Eurasian Plate

Juan de Fuca Plate

Arabian Plate

Philippine Plate

Caribbean Plate

Cocos Plate

Pacific Plate

Indo-Australian Plate

Nazca Plate

African Plate

South American Plate

Antarctic Plate

Scotia Plate

⬅ Direction of plate movement

© 2007 EB Inc.

The giant plates that make up Earth's crust move in different directions.

plates move toward each other. The edge of one plate may slide alongside another. Or they may crash into each other. Plates slide mostly because of magma temperature changes and gravity. They move about 2 to 4 inches (5 to 10 centimeters) every year. These plates have been moving for hundreds of millions of years.

 Deep canyons on land or under the ocean often form when Earth's plates move apart.

MOUNTAINS

Over millions of years, the movement of plates forced these mountain layers to bend.

Mountains can form when two plates collide. When the plates push against each other hard enough, mountains of metamorphic rock fold upward. They may be forced up to form very high mountain ranges on land. The pressure that forces the rocks to move also changes their minerals. Regional metamorphism is the process of creating metamorphic rocks when mountains are being formed. Over millions of years, the pressure of the plates pushes land together and moves mountain ranges toward the sky.

Think About It

What happens to rocks when water is forced out during metamorphism?

Nearly all of the world's major mountain ranges are made up of mostly metamorphic rock. The Rockies, Andes, and Himalayas began forming between 60 and 70 million years ago. The Himalayas were formed when the Indian subcontinent collided into the Eurasian plate. The Appalachians and Urals formed more than 250 million years ago.

Mountain ranges filled with metamorphic rock are made when plates push together.

SHOCKINGLY FAST

Most metamorphic rock formed from pressure and heat over millions of years. However, sometimes metamorphic rock can change at the speed of light. When lightning strikes sand in a desert, the tiny grains may fuse together immediately and become a metamorphic rock called fulgurite. This process is called shock metamorphism. Fulgurite breaks easily because it is not strong. It is hard but similar to glass in strength.

Shock, or impact, metamorphism can

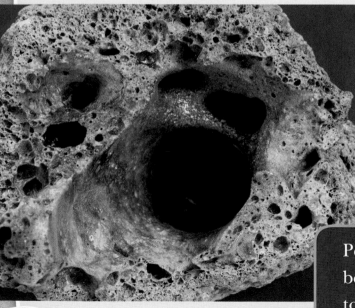

People value and collect fulgurite because it is an unusual rock and hard to find. This example is like a glassy hollow tube.

Compare and Contrast

How are the surfaces of moons and planets similar to the surfaces on Earth?

also happen when meteorites hit the surface of Earth. Meteorites are rocks from space. When a meteorite falls through Earth's atmosphere, it creates a lot of heat. When the meteorite crashes into the ground, the rocky layers close to the surface can become metamorphic rock right away.

At about 60 tons, the Hoba meteorite in Namibia is the largest known meteorite found on Earth.

GNEISS AND SLATE

The most common metamorphic rock is gneiss (pronounced "nice"). It is also some of the oldest metamorphic rock.

Some gneiss is more than three billion years old. Gneiss formed when great heat and pressure changed the structure of granite, an igneous rock. The shrinking and pressure pushed the minerals into tight bands of light and dark colors. Gneiss is hard and tough.

Another common metamorphic rock is slate. Slate forms from shale, which in turn is formed from the clay

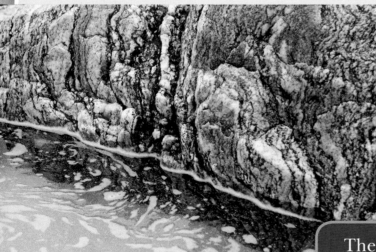

The minerals in gneiss create beautiful lines of gray, black, brown, white, or other colors.

Slate is mined in many sizes to make materials for flooring and roofing.

sediments of rivers and lakes pressed together under low temperature and pressure.

When shale is pressed hard enough with high heat for millions of years, it changes into slate. This metamorphic rock comes in gray, blue, green, purple, or red. People can easily cut slate into flat tiles for roofs, floors, and sidewalks.

SCHIST

Slate changes to phyllite, a new metamorphic rock when pressed and baked. With even more heat and pressure, phyllite can change into schist, also a metamorphic rock. Schist is a dark, shiny rock. The mineral crystals grow larger with each change. Schist is one of the more common metamorphic rocks in North America. The name "schist" comes from Greek words meaning "to split."

Some schist rocks contain garnets or other well-known minerals. Garnets are usually red, but they also come in such colors as purple, yellow,

When slate is heated and subjected to pressure, it can become a new rock called phyllite.

Gemstones are minerals that, when cut and polished, can be used in jewelry.

green, orange, or even clear. Garnets are hard crystals. They are cut into beautiful gemstones and added to rings, earrings, necklaces, and other jewelry. Garnets are also used to make sandpaper.

Lovely crystals of garnet have bright and clear colors and are valued as jewelry.

21

MARBLE AND QUARTZITE

One of the most widely used metamorphic rocks is marble. This rock forms from limestone, a sedimentary rock rich in calcium. The calcium comes from sea shells built up in the oceans and changed to limestone. Under pressure and high temperature, limestone becomes marble.

People prize marble because it is beautiful and strong. They can cut and shape it into sculptures and buildings. This stone is often white, but it can also be black, red, or green.

Marble is found in mountains around the world. Greece is famous for its white marble.

←

Quartzite is a tough metamorphic rock. People use this hard rock to build roads and as materials for roofs. It formed when sandstone, a sedimentary rock, was changed by heat and pressure inside Earth. The stone comes in white, pink, or gray. It is so hard that it can scratch glass.

Think About It

Harmful gases from factories and motor vehicles affect marble statues and buildings. What do you think happens to marble over time?

Artists use white marble more than other rocks to carve sculptures because it cuts easily.

FOLIATED AND NONFOLIATED ROCKS

Metamorphic rocks can look very different from one another. Great heat and pressure change their minerals into different crystal structures. Metamorphic rock can be identified by its appearance and feel, called texture. The two main types of texture are foliated and nonfoliated. Rocks with a foliated texture have minerals in wavy lines or stripes or can be separated into layers. Slate, schist, and gneiss are foliated metamorphic rocks. Nonfoliated metamorphic rocks

Rocks and mountains with foliated texture form from high heat and pressure.

Compare and Contrast

Slate is a foliated rock with distinct layers. What do you think slate looks like after falling off a steep cliff?

have one or just a few minerals in them that are hard to see. These rocks have a smooth texture and often have been changed from heat or low pressure over a long time. Marble is a nonfoliated metamorphic rock formed from limestone. Hornfels is another nonfoliated rock. It forms when shale comes in contact with very hot magma. People use hornfels to build roads.

This rock cliff in Japan is very smooth and hard. It is made from the mineral hornfels.

IDENTIFYING METAMORPHIC ROCKS

It can be difficult to tell the difference between metamorphic rock and the two other types of rock (igneous and sedimentary). Geologists may study the crystals in a rock. Their color

Vocabulary

Scientists who study rocks and minerals are called geologists.

Geologists around the world work to discover new metamorphic rocks and ways to use them.

and hardness help geologists identify the minerals in the rock. Some minerals occur only in metamorphic rocks. Other minerals, such as garnet, appear most commonly in metamorphic rocks.

Geologists also look at the texture of rocks to identify the different types. Metamorphic rocks do not have pores, or small openings, as sedimentary rocks do. They also do not have the remains of living creatures that sedimentary rocks may have. Foliated metamorphic rocks can be identified by the banding, or clearly visible layers of the different minerals within the rocks.

When geologists are exploring, they can use the quick streak test to identify rocks. This rock is magnetite.

MANY USES

Metamorphic rocks are common. The rocks often contain minerals not found in other rocks. The minerals can withstand very high temperatures and are strong. Ancient people used quartzite to make tools. Today, metamorphic rocks are used to make buildings, garden walks, and roads. People also use minerals in metamorphic rocks to make jewelry.

Ancient knives and axes made from quartzite have a sharp cutting edge and strong, hard points.

Compare and Contrast

Compare why metamorphic rocks are better for building materials than sedimentary rocks such as limestone.

Metamorphic rock is one of the three major types of rock and is an important part of Earth. It is the only rock formed by great pressure and very high heat over millions of years. The appearance, location, and minerals of metamorphic rocks provide information about changes above and below Earth's surface. The study of metamorphic rocks helps geologists understand how the Earth's crust moves over time.

Roofs made from metamorphic slate keep out water and last for a very long time.

GLOSSARY

atmospheric pressure The weight of the air.

contact metamorphism When metamorphic rocks are created from the high temperatures of magma.

crust The thin, rocky layer on the surface of Earth.

Eurasian plate A large, moving piece of solid rock of Earth's outer layer that is made up of Europe and Asia.

foliated Rocks that have minerals in wavy lines or stripes and are able to be separated into layers. Slate, schist, and gneiss are foliated metamorphic rocks.

magma Hot liquid rock that forms below the surface of Earth.

mantle The middle layer of Earth that is between the crust and the core.

metamorphic rocks Rocks that form when heat, pressure, or both cause changes in rock.

minerals A solid that has an ordered atomic structure. Minerals make up Earth's rocks, sands, and soils.

plates The large, moving pieces of solid rock that make up Earth's outer layer.

regional metamorphism When metamorphic rocks are created by high pressure over a very large area.

temperature The measurement of how hot or cold something is.

texture The structure, feel, and appearance of something.

FOR MORE INFORMATION

BOOKS

Lawrence, Ellen. *Baking and Crushing: A Look at Metamorphic Rock.* New York, NY: Bearport Publishing, 2015.

Nelson, Maria. *Metamorphic Rocks* (That Rocks!). New York, NY: Gareth Stevens Publishing, 2014.

Oxlade, Chris. *Metamorphic Rocks* (Let's Rock). Chicago, IL: Heinemann, 2011.

Swanson, Jennifer. *Metamorphic Rocks* (Rocks and Minerals). Minneapolis, MN: Core Library, 2015.

WEBSITES

Because of the changing nature of Internet links, Rosen Publishing has developed an online list of websites related to the subject of this book. This site is updated regularly. Please use this link to access the list:

http://www.rosenlinks.com/GEOL/Meta

INDEX